CHARLES E. IVES

POSTLUDE IN F

for Organ

(reconstructed by Charles Krigbaum)

AMP-8074

First printing: November 1994

Associated Music Publishers, Inc.

DISTRIBUTED BY

HAL•LEONARD™
CORPORATION

7777 W. BLUEMOUND RD. P.O. BOX 13819 MILWAUKEE, WI 53213

Performance Notes

The first time I heard Charles Ives' *Postlude in F* was from a CD, *The Orchestral Music of Charles Ives*, played by the Orchestra of New England, James Sinclair, conductor. Because it was a premiere recording, it aroused my curiosity. The music suggested that it was an early work, Wagnerian in style, and the title indicated an original setting for organ.

Kenneth Singleton, an Ives scholar, has written an interesting preface to it: ". . . composed in 1895, [it] is Charles Ives' earliest known work for large orchestra. It is based on an earlier organ piece which Ives performed at the Baptist Church in Danbury, Connecticut on May 11, 1890 (at the age of fifteen). The version for orchestra was probably produced as an orchestration assignment for a class of Horatio Parker, Ives' teacher at Yale College. Ives recalled that the "New Haven Orchestra" (the New Haven Symphony Orchestra, organized by Parker in 1895) read through the work in 1896. The *Postlude in F,* which was also preparation for work on the *First Symphony* (its first movement also completed in 1895), contains some surprisingly mature and beautiful writing, especially in the magical closing pages."

Because the original organ version was lost and James Sinclair had persuasively advocated its recreation, I have attempted to produce a version that would work on the organ. Originally I wanted to write for a simple church instrument of the period, but later it seemed more in accordance with Ives' spirit to make use of the full resources of the Newberry Memorial organ at Yale University where I performed the work in September of 1992.

Whatever the instrument, it is important to keep a balance between solo and accompanying material. To do this best, I recommend following the French system of using Jeux de Fonds (essentially Montre 8, Bourdon 8, Flute Harmonique 8, Gamba 8) or some such equivalent on each manual, with perhaps an occasional Flute 4, especially if it is a harmonic flute. Coupling all the divisions ensures a pyramidal structure of similar sounds, graded dynamically. If one is lucky enough to have a fourth manual with reeds and unenclosed tuba and/or trumpet, follow the suggestions listed below.

If one has a three-manual organ and no large solo reed, it is advisable to move down one notch in this pyramidal system, that is, substitute Great for Solo, and Choir for Great whenever the figuration cannot be played on a single manual. For example, in m. 35, you may keep both hands on the Great or play the accompanimental figuration on the choir with the left hand while playing the solo material on the Great. Similarly, in m. 60, one could simply add a large reed or several powerful stops on the downbeat, reducing a bit on the second eighth note of m. 63 and moving the right hand down to the Choir manual wherever convenient. If possible, reduce the Swell greatly at the end of the piece, even to single Flute 8 or Flute Celeste.

There are a few spots in this reconstruction that are difficult to perform. These are due primarily to the contrapuntal (solo versus accompaniment) nature of the music and to octave doublings, many of which I have retained from the orchestral score. Some of these are not essential, however, and if they cause technical problems, can be omitted.

One final suggestion: play this piece as Wagner suggests in his essay on conducting, that is, with flexible tempos. It is in the romantic style. Expand phrases, linger if appropriate, and above all, play expressively.

—CHARLES KRIGBAUM

Registrational Suggestions:
Pd Foundation Stops 16 and 8
Sw Foundation Stops 8
Ch Foundation Stops 8 and Flute 4
Gt Foundation Stops 8 and Flute 4
So Foundation Stops 8, Flute 4
    (Trumpet and Tuba 8 if under expression)
Sw, Ch and Gt/Pd; Sw, Ch, Gt/So; Sw and Ch/Gt; Sw/Ch

duration: ca. 5 minutes

This version of Postlude in F *was premiered on September 20, 1992 at Woolsey Hall,*
The Yale School of Music, New Haven, Connecticut with Charles Krigbaum, organ.

A critical edition (full score and parts) of the orchestral version is available for purchase, order number 50481114. The score may also be purchased separately, order number 50481195.

POSTLUDE IN F

Charles E. Ives
(reconstructed by Charles Krigbaum)

Moderato, broadly and lyrically

2